BE Z.O.E.

First Second Third John

Εἰμί ζωή

Ages 8 – 10

Zealous Obedient Expectant

MaryBeth Clare

Be Z.O.E. Ages 8-10
is available at special quantity discounts for bulk purchase for sales promotions,
premiums, fund-raising, and educational needs.
For details write Endurance Press, 577 N Cardigan Ave, Star, ID 83669.

Visit Endurance Press' website at www.endurancepress.com

Be Z.O.E. Ages 8-10

PUBLISHED BY ENDURANCE PRESS
577 N Cardigan Ave
Star, ID 83669 U.S.A.

All rights reserved. Except for brief excerpts for review purposes,
no part of this book may be
reproduced or used in any form without
prior written permission from the publisher.

ISBN 978-0-998875682

®2019 MaryBeth Clare

Cover by Teal Rose Design Studios

Interior & Cover art by Darin Eason

Printed in the United States of America

First Edition 2019

Table of Contents

Introduction..Page 6-8

Week 1: Jesus Explains the Brazen Serpent...............Page 9-20
Numbers 21:5-9, John 3:1-21

Week 2: Living in the Light..Page 21-32
1st John 1

Week 3: Jesus, Our Advocate, Our Propitiation.........Page 33-43
1st John 2

Week 4: Gods' Great Love..Page 44-54
1st John 3

Week 5: A Time of Testing...Page 55-65
1st John 4

Week 6: Be Assured...Page 66-76
1st John 5

Week 7: Be Aware..Page 77-87
2nd John

Week 8: Lessons From the Good and the Bad...........Page 88-98
3rd John

End Notes..Page 99

Introduction

Welcome to Be Z.O.E.. Dr. James Strong paved the way for those of us who aren't Hebrew, Greek, or Aramaic scholars to study the Word in its original languages. In 1890, the first edition of Strong's Concordance was published. He gave us the definitions for every word in the original texts. These will be what I reference in our word studies. H is for Hebrew found mainly in the Old Testament. G is for Greek, and A is for Aramaic, these two are mainly in the New Testament. Dr. Strong used the King James translation (KJV).

The Greek word for life is ZOE. There are three characteristics which are prudent to apply to our daily lives:

***Z** - Zealous, G2207: To most eagerly desire.*

We need to desire our relationship with God on a daily basis. We can do this through prayer, journaling, being in the Word, fellowship, and the list goes on.

***O** - Obedient, G5219: To listen, to submit.*

God has a plan and purpose for each person. When He created you, He thought of all the plans He had in store for you. We need to seek Him (through being Zealous) and ask Him what He requires of us daily. It could be a little thing, or working on a dream you've had for many years. Within this we must be obedient to His calling, even when we might not understand. You will know His direction for your life as it lines up with the Word. He will not ask you to do something that ever goes against the Word.

***E** - Expectant, H6960: To wait, to look for, to hope.*

One thing we are always to look for is our Messiah calling us home in the rapture. He can come at any moment and we are to be expectant. When we look to being expectant in daily life, God has many surprises for us throughout our lives. We need to be expectant of what He wants to do, and look for the opportunities He brings to us.

Each week can be done in a group or individually. Each week contains seven sub-sections:

1. At the start of each week you'll have a leader's overview. This is here to help any parent/leader know what the key points in the lesson are.

2. Each lesson begins with Bible reading. It's very important to be in the Bible at every age. Write out three things you learned.

3. Next we take a deeper look. We will discuss some history, explain some words in their original language and talk about how you can apply it to your daily life.

4. Seeing Z.O.E reflected. It's time to take an in-depth look at the lives of people from the Bible and how they show these three characteristics.

5. Here we have a memory verse and being Z.O.E.

6. Now it's time for some fun. You will have a few puzzles that relate back to your lesson.

7. Each week ends with writing out a prayer to God.

Through all the studies we will talk a lot about salvation. There are three parts to salvation:

1. Justification: Jesus died and rose again for your sins. Through this your sins have been forgiven and you are justified.

2. Sanctification: The Holy Spirit wants to work in and through you. He will mold you into the image of Jesus. This process takes a lifetime. It is all about our growth in the Lord.

3. Glorification: This one will happen when we get to Heaven. We will have our glorified bodies. We will be permanently removed from the presence of sin!

You are a beautiful creation of God. He has a plan and purpose for you. By being in the Bible and learning how it applies to your life, you are delighting God. He is smiling over you. Before starting your study, please pray and ask the Holy Spirit to reveal truth to you.

It is my prayer that this will bring you closer to your Creator.

God's richest blessing, and may He bring you much joy,

MaryBeth

Week 1

Jesus Explains the Brazen Serpent

Leader/Parent Overview

The books of First, Second, and Third John are written to those who believe. Before we embark upon them it is vital for kids to understand sin, salvation, and Jesus' free gift of salvation. This is the focus for this chapter.

Key points:

- Sin is disobedience to God and what He has commanded us.
- All humans sin.
- Sin separates God and humans.
- Jesus came to bring humans and God back together.
- Jesus is part of God. You can explain that God is God the Father, God the Son, and God the Holy Spirit - The Trinity.
- Jesus loves you so much that He died, was buried, and lived again on the third day.
- Jesus' gift is free, we cannot do anything to earn it, and it is open to every person.
- Accepting His gift is asking Jesus into your heart. It means that you and God are no longer separated.
- The Holy Spirit comes and lives inside you and helps you to live a life that makes God happy.

Additional Questions:

- What does it mean to disobey?
- What does it mean to love someone?
- How can you show someone you love them? How can you show Jesus you love Him?

Jesus Explains the Brazen Serpent

This week please read the passages below and write down three things you learn.

Numbers 21: 5-9 "The Bronze Serpent Raised"

1. _____
_____
_____

2. _____
_____
_____

3. _____
_____
_____

John 3:1-21 "Salvation open to all who will believe"

1. _____
_____
_____

2. _____
_____
_____

3. _____
_____
_____

Taking A Deeper Look

In our first passage we meet a man named Moses. He is a man who loved and served God. In the book of Exodus we find out that he was the one God sent to Pharaoh in order to free God's people, the Jewish people, from the land of Egypt. After the people were freed from slavery in Egypt they grumbled against God a lot. They did it so much that God said that none of that generation, with the exception of two people, would enter God's promised land. Instead of going to the land, they ended up walking around in a desert for 40 years. It is during this forty year period that we hear them grumbling once again. In our first passage, the people spoke against God and Moses. They grumbled and complained saying there is no bread, or water, and they didn't like what they did have. By this time God had enough of their complaining. He sent fiery serpents to the wilderness. The venom in these snakes was so powerful it would kill a person with just one bite. This got the attention of the Jewish people fast. They went to Moses, told him that they had sinned by grumbling and complaining about God and Moses. Then they asked for Moses to pray to God on their behalf. God gave Moses specific instructions on what he was to do. Moses then followed what God said and made a bronze serpent which was set on a pole. Moses told the people that if they didn't want to die after being bitten they had to look to the serpent and they would live. There are some good lessons we can learn from this. First, grumbling and complaining makes God sad. Do you know what else makes Him sad? Talking bad about others, just like the Jewish people did in this passage. This isn't the type of behavior God wants His kids to participate in. The Bible tells us that we are to love one another. Matthew 7:12 tells us that we are to treat others the way we want to be treated.

1. How do you want to be treated? How do you treat others?

_____
_____
_____
_____

2. Why does grumbling, complaining, or talking bad about others make God sad? Why is it bad behavior?

_____

_____

_____

_____

    Now let's move on to John 3. We meet a man named Nicodemus. He is a very curious man. He likes to ask questions so he can learn. One day he meets Jesus and asks Him a lot of questions. Before he asks anything he tells Jesus that he is sure that He is a teacher from God because of all the great miracles He is doing. Jesus replied that no man can see God unless he is born again! You might be wondering the same thing that Nicodemus asked, "How can a man be born a second time? It's not like he can go back into his mothers womb!" Jesus answered by saying that this second birth is one of the spirit, it is a spiritual birth. Jesus followed up his answer by reminding Nicodemus about Moses and the bronze serpent. Then Jesus continued and told him that likewise the Son of God would be lifted up and anyone who wants to have everlasting life must look to Him.

    All humans sin. Sin happens when we are being disobedient to God. The first time sin entered the world was with Adam and Eve. God told them not to eat of the tree of Knowledge of Good and Evil, and they did it anyway. After this happened God made a sacrifice and covered Adam and Eve.[1] Later on, God gave the nation of Israel many commands and instructions regarding sacrifices. They did sacrifices until 70 A.D. when their temple was destroyed.

    Here's some good news. God had a plan long before He created the Heavens and Earth.[2] He sent Jesus, God's Son, to die for our sins. Jesus offered Himself as a sacrifice. When He lived here on Earth He never sinned. He was innocent of all guilt when He died. He died, was buried, rose again, then later on He ascended into Heaven.[3] Now we can have life through His gift of salvation. There is nothing you can do to earn it, He just wants to give it to you. All you have to do is say yes and accept it.

    When Jesus answers Nicodemus' question, Jesus says one must be born again. In the Greek, again, means from above.[4] When you accept Jesus' free gift of salvation you are born from above. You have a spiritual birth.

Seeing Z.O.E. Reflected in this Passage

Z - God is Zealous for you and wants to be your friend. He has reached out and said "I love you and want to be your friend" through Jesus' gift of salvation. Have you accepted this gift? If not, do you want to accept it?

_____
_____
_____
_____
_____

O - Jesus was Obedient in His life. He followed all of God's rules. What are some of God's rules that you are good at following? Are there some you find harder to follow?

_____
_____
_____
_____
_____

E - 1st John 1:9 tells us that when we repent, tell God we are sorry, that He is ready and willing to forgive. When we repent we can Expect God will forgive us. Is there anything you need to repent of today?

_____
_____
_____
_____
_____

Memory Verse

"For I am not ashamed of the gospel, for it is the power of God for salvation to everyone who believes, to the Jew first and also to the Greek."

Romans 1:16

The Gospel is that Jesus died, was buried, and rose again. Do you believe this? If so, how do you share the Gospel with your friends and others?

_____
_____
_____
_____
_____

Being Z.O.E.

This week we saw how Nicodemus learned a lot through asking questions. What are some questions you have? This week I want you to do two things:

- Pray and tell God some of your questions. Go to your Bible, look in the concordance (it's in the back of your Bible) to find different passages that talk about whatever your question is. Read the passages and write down any answers. For instance if you want to know more about salvation, look up the word salvation.

- Find a trustworthy adult that has accepted Jesus' free gift and ask them some of your questions.

_____
_____
_____
_____

Jesus Explains The Brazen Serpent

```
G Q Z Z G F R F B X H S F V B
N R L U F W Y P G X F D O O P
I C U L T H Q T D B O Q R L M
C S M M L E R N F R C R G Y O
O W X K B H M I J O Y U I U S
D P A G D L X P X N G U V E E
E F B Z E R I L M Z Z E E P S
M D N G X A Q N K E L G H D M
U R J B V Q D O G M R R V Y Y
S N F E W L W A H R I W O R M
O W L U S D M C M R T X Y D R
M F O S K U X R T V D O W I M
S I N G P A S I J F R R Z U S
C F C V U Z B Y N A L S L E F
I A K E V E Q U M M G A Z A M
```

ADAM	BRONZE	EVE
FORGIVE	GRUMBLING	JESUS
MOSES	NICODEMUS	SIN

Jesus Explains The Brazen Serpent

Across

2) God is ready and willing to do this when we repent
4) God's Son
7) A man who asked Jesus a lot of questions

Down

1) The man who spoke to God on behalf of Israel
3) Similar to complaining
5) The first man
6) The color of the serpent Moses made
8) The first woman
9) Something all humans do

Jesus Explains The Brazen Serpent

Directions: Match the numbers to the letters to reveal the answer

A	B	C	D	E	F	G	H	I	J	K	L	M
1	2	3	4	5	6	7	8	9	10	11	12	13

N	O	P	Q	R	S	T	U	V	W	X	Y	Z
14	15	16	17	18	19	20	21	22	23	24	25	26

The first humans were ____ ____ ____ ____ and ____ ____ ____. They
                                   1   4   1   13   5   22   5

____ ____ ____ ____ ____ ____ ____ ____ ____ ____ ____ ____.
 4   9   19   15   2   5   25   5   4   7   15   4

Sin causes a ____ ____ ____ ____ ____ ____ between ____ ____ ____
               4   9   22   9   4   5   7   15   4

and ____ ____ ____ ____ ____ ____. Since God loves us He sent
     8   21   13   1   14   19

____ ____ ____ ____ ____, His ____ ____ ____.
10   5   19   21   19   19   15   14

Jesus ____ ____ ____ ____, was ____ ____ ____ ____ ____ ____ and
       4   9   5   4   2   21   18   9   5   4

____ ____ ____ ____   ____ ____ ____ ____ ____!
18   15   19   5   1   7   1   9   14

Dear God,

Your Friend,

Week 2

Living in the Light

Leader/Parent Overview

Key Points:

- Jesus was a human just like you and me. He felt all the emotions we feel, had a family, and grew up. One of the big differences is that He lived a perfect life. He never sinned. It is because of this that He was able to bring God and humans back together.

- Once we accept Jesus' free gift of salvation we no longer choose or have a desire to sin. We will sin but it is not something that we will make a habit of doing. Instead we want to tell the truth and live according to God's commandments.

- John tells us that once we accept Jesus' free gift we are in fellowship with God. This means that we are partners (literally in the Greek) with God. Some kids might better understand this being described as friendship. He does things for us and we do things for Him.

Additional Questions:

- What is a lie? What is truth? What is the difference between truths and lies?

- What is a habit? How can you make telling the truth a habit?

- What are some things God has done for you? What are some things you have done for God?

- How can you be God's partner/friend?

Living in the Light

Bible Reading

This week please read the following passage and write down three things you learn.

1st John 1

1. _____
   _____
   _____
   _____
   _____

2. _____
   _____
   _____
   _____
   _____
   _____

3. _____
   _____
   _____
   _____
   _____

Taking A Deeper Look

John is the writer of the letters we will be diving into. He also wrote a Gospel. He was the youngest of Jesus' disciples being only a teenager when he decided to begin his walk with the Lord. After Jesus' death, he took care of His mom, Mary. They lived in Ephesus. Ephesus was a big city filled with people of all different beliefs and there were a lot of people there who didn't believe in Jesus.

John was the Elder, or the Pastor, of the church in Ephesus. Churches back then aren't like our churches today. There weren't a lot of church buildings with different denominations and you could pick and choose which one you would go to. When the believers all got together, they met in each other's houses. They would talk about all different things they had learned from Jesus and read Scripture from the Old Testament. The New Testament was still being written at that time.

In John's first letter he reminds the people in his church about the facts of Jesus. They heard Jesus teach, they saw Him with their own eyes, some of them even touched Him! This was important to remind them of because some of those who were against Jesus taught that Jesus didn't really exist.

Further on John tells them that they had Fellowship with Jesus. Since Jesus is a part of the Triune God, that means that they had fellowship with God. The Greek word fellowship means that they are in a joint partnership.[5] This means they are partners with God and in His plan! My Friend, if you have accepted Jesus' free gift of salvation, you too are in fellowship with God. He will use you for His plan!

1. What does it mean to you to be in a partnership with God? Partners work together to make something better. What can you do for God today?

_____
_____
_____
_____

In the second half of this chapter John tells us that God is light and in Him there is no darkness. We, as God's friends, and partakers in His plan, need to be light shining in a dark world. What do we mean by dark? Well, one could love sinning and disobeying God. Another could love bullying other kids around and showing hate toward others. These things are things that God tells us not to do. We are to live by God's rules and the most important of those rules are all about love. By being in the dark means that someone wants to do the opposite of what God commands us. If we are His partakers, we need to really make sure we follow God's rules. Certainly, we all will mess up from time to time but the key difference is we don't make a habit of it. Moreover, when we do sin, we repent. In our repentance God comes and forgives us.

2. How can you be a bright light shining for God?

_____
_____
_____
_____
_____

Seeing Z.O.E. Reflected in this Passage

Z - God is so zealous for us to be right with Him that He is always ready to forgive, all we have to do is ask. We should be ready to forgive those who hurt us. By doing this we are being obedient and it shows God that we are zealous to be like Him. Is there anyone you need to forgive?

_____
_____
_____
_____
_____

O - One way we can be Obedient is by being God's light in a dark world. Write down three ways we can show God's light and contrast them with their opposite. For instance kindness versus bullying.

_____
_____
_____
_____
_____

E - Think of your partnership/fellowship with God like a friendship. How do you Expect your friends to treat you? How do you treat your friends? Do you Expect your friends to like or participate in activities that you enjoy? How can you apply this example to your friendship with God?

_____
_____
_____
_____
_____

Memory Verse

"And the Scripture was fulfilled that says, "Abraham believed God, and it was counted to him as righteousness"—and he was called a friend of God."
James 2:23

God made a very special promise to Abraham. When it didn't look like it would come to pass, Abraham still believed God. God has promises that He has made to all of us that we can find in the Bible. He also makes special promises to each of us individually.

Do you believe that God will keep all of His promises? Why or why not? Take it a step further, do you believe your friends will keep their promises to you? Do you keep the promises you make to your friends? Remember, Abraham believed, was righteous, and was called God's friend.

_____
_____
_____
_____
_____

Being Z.O.E.

This week look up each of these references and write out the promise God has given you.

Romans 8:1

_____
_____
_____
_____
_____

Romans 10:9

_____
_____
_____
_____
_____

Philippians 4:19

_____
_____
_____
_____
_____

1st John 1:9

_____
_____
_____
_____
_____

Living In The Light

```
X H B Q I F S Y P O H W N E L
D M O T L C K V P Z U N N U I
W P R M P X E F S D G E X A G
B A M H E I I P A X C J G C H
S R O K X S C P H P R V F U T
G T L L S E E L R E U B N X V
G N K V N D M Y R W S A R P E
H E L H I H P G U U A U R F O
T R K Z F P C Y A J M G S X D
S S H S N W J B Q J L Q D B J
P H E D P K R X N Y X V A L S
P I A F P F H N Y V B I R H I
H P R L N H N A M M X E K Z N
D T R U T H B Y P G C J M D Q
U L I C V X W I N P M T U B L
```

DARK　　　　EPHESUS　　　　HEAR

HOMES　　　　LIGHT　　　　PARTNERSHIP

SEE　　　　SIN　　　　TRUTH

Living In The Light

Across

4) Opposite of light
5) Opposite of dark
6) In the New Testament, Christians met in _____ for their service
7) You do this with your eyes
8) Opposite of a lie

Down

1) John is the elder of the church in _____
2) The meaning of the Greek word fellowship
3) What we need to repent of
6) You do this with your ears

Living In The Light

Directions: Match the numbers to the letters to reveal the answer

A	B	C	D	E	F	G	H	I	J	K	L	M
1	2	3	4	5	6	7	8	9	10	11	12	13

N	O	P	Q	R	S	T	U	V	W	X	Y	Z
14	15	16	17	18	19	20	21	22	23	24	25	26

__ __ __ __ was the __ __ __ __ __ __ at the
10 15 8 14   16 1 19 20 15 18

church in __ __ __ __ __ __ __
          5 16 8 5 19 21 19

There are many __ __ __ __ __ __ __ __
               23 9 20 14 5 19 19 5 19

to the __ __ __ __ , __ __ __ __ __ , and
       12 9 6 5   4 5 1 20 8

__ __ __ __ __ __ __ __ __ __ __ of
18 5 19 21 18 18 5 3 20 9 15 14

__ __ __ __ __
10 5 19 21 19

As God's __ __ __ __ __ __ '__ we are to
         6 18 9 5 14 4   19

__ __ __ __ in His __ __ __ __ __
12 9 22 5   12 9 7 8 20

Dear God,

Your Friend,

Week 3

Jesus, Our Advocate, Our Propitiation

Leader/Parent Overview

Key Points:

- Understand the difference between Advocate and Propitiation. Often these words are thought to be synonymous but they're not.

- An Advocate is a person. It is one who comes to one's aid.

- Propitiation is usually a verb. It is an action that is done in order to appease/stop the wrath of another.

- In our case Jesus is our Advocate. Through His completed work on the cross He brought propitiation. He appeased the wrath of God through His sacrifice.

- Explain God's two greatest commandments: Love God with your heart, mind, soul, and strength. Second, love your neighbor as yourself.

- We can look to Jesus as our example in living these out perfectly.

Additional Questions:

- How did Jesus love God with all of Himself?
- How did Jesus show love to you?
- How does the Holy Spirit help you to love others?
- What are some kind, loving actions we can express toward others?

Jesus, Our Advocate, Our Propitiation

Bible Reading

This week please read the following passage and write down three things you learn.

1st John 2

1. _____

2. _____

3. _____

Taking A Deeper Look

This chapter is filled with many good lessons. We are going to focus on two. The first one focuses on two words that are given to describe Jesus: Advocate and Propitiation. An Advocate is someone who gives help to someone in need.[6] An example of an advocate are charities. Charity organizations pick a cause or someone in need and help them out. There are some for homeless folks, others for people who cannot afford food, some for people with various illnesses and diseases.

Next we see the word propitiation. This is a big word that simply means to make someone who is angry not angry anymore.[7] For instance, let's say a friend of yours is really mean to you. This makes you feel hurt and extremely angry. Then another friend comes along, talks with you about it and this talk helps you to reason it out and helps you to not be angry anymore. Let's see how we can apply this to Jesus.

In our case we have sinned. Sin makes God sad and angry because it separates us from Him. He wants to have communication with us and be a part of our lives. He is angry with the sin that causes the divide. Jesus, God's Son, came to be our Advocate and bring a propitiation for our sins.

We need an Advocate because we have sinned. Jesus comes and stands before God and says "Yes, that person is covered in my blood and can have fellowship with us." In this He is standing up for us which is what an Advocate does and He is appeasing God's anger by saying that we are now covered in His blood.

1. In your own words describe what an Advocate does and how propitiation works.

_____
_____
_____
_____
_____

2. How do you feel knowing that Jesus is your advocate and made things right so you can have fellowship with God?

_____
_____
_____
_____
_____

There are two great commands in the Bible. God's commands are rules by which we should live. Jesus said that the two greatest are: to love God with all your heart, mind, soul, and strength and the second is: to love your neighbor as yourself.[8] Even though these two commands are old and were given a long time ago, John tells us they are new! He says this because Jesus lived them out perfectly. He loved God with all of Him and never placed anyone or anything above His relationship with God. He also lived out loving one's neighbor. By neighbor he doesn't mean just those whom you live close by, he means all people. We can love and extend love toward others because God loves us.

3. How do you love God with all of you? How do you extend love toward others?

_____
_____
_____
_____
_____

Seeing Z.O.E. Reflected in this Passage

Z - We can show God we are Zealous for Him by living out His two greatest rules. What is the hardest part for you in living these out? What comes easy?

_____
_____
_____
_____
_____

O - Jesus is a perfect example of Obedience. He gives us the Holy Spirit to help us live a life filled with Obedience. How do you make sure you're Obedient in your life?

_____
_____
_____
_____
_____

E - God is love. He loves everyone, even those who do not love Him. He Expects us to show love toward others also. What are some ways you extend love toward others? On the flip side, what are some ways others have extended love to you?

_____
_____
_____
_____
_____

Memory Verse

"But the Helper, the Holy Spirit, whom the Father will send in my name, he will teach you all things and bring to your remembrance all that I have said to you."

John 14:26

In this passage Jesus is talking with some of His disciples. He tells them that one day He must leave but another will come. He is referring to the Holy Spirit. He even says that the Holy Spirit is an Advocate! The Holy Spirit helps us to remember things that Jesus taught and helps us to live a life that will make God happy.

How do you see the Holy Spirit at work in your life?

_____
_____
_____
_____
_____

Being Z.O.E.

Everyday this week do something kind or loving for someone. It can be as simple as holding a door open, smiling when someone frowns at you, doing a chore without being asked. There are many ways you can do this. Write down what you did.

_____
_____
_____
_____
_____

Jesus, Our Advocate and Propitiation

```
F C M F K K M T G K X S F H R
X P O O Y F E W T C X W J T C
S D V M U O Y B H S A S N K P
C E F T M S U K T O B O N C R
C I J R I A N R C X T G E B O
P O I N K R N D S A O T I N P
H P V A M G M D H E L A G A I
O K N E O N Z K S Z L P H V T
S V B D R P I E S U X F B I I
B B K M T S V K U M C H O T A
V W Q A D V O C A T E H R P T
M Y L Y I L K O L W B D S U I
W H S T W L R R Y S Z N R U O
L Y F M S E P A R A T E S V N
D I S C I P L E S V D E T N V
```

ADVOCATE	COMMANDS	COVERS
DISCIPLES	ME	NEIGHBORS
PROPITIATION	SEPARATES	YOURSELF

Jesus, Our Advocate and Propitiation

Across

3) All people, not just those who live near you
5) Love God with all of ____
7) Love your neighbor as _____
8) Someone who represents someone in need
9) Sin _____ us from God

Down

1) Jesus had 12 of these
2) Jesus' blood _____ our sins
4) To make someone not angry
6) God's rule

Jesus, Our Advocate and Propitiation

Directions: Match the numbers to the letters to reveal the answer

A	B	C	D	E	F	G	H	I	J	K	L	M
1	2	3	4	5	6	7	8	9	10	11	12	13

N	O	P	Q	R	S	T	U	V	W	X	Y	Z
14	15	16	17	18	19	20	21	22	23	24	25	26

___ ___ ___ ___ ___ ___ ___ ___ ___ ___ ___ ___
16 18 15 16 9   20 9   1   20 9   15 14

takes away ___ ___ ___ ___ ___
           1   14 7   5   18

An ___ ___ ___ ___ ___ ___ ___ ___ ___ ___ ___ ___ ___'___
   1   4   22 15 3   1   20 5   8   5   12 16 19

___ ___ ___ ___ ___ ___ ___ ___ ___ ___ ___
20 8   15 19 5   9   14   14 5   5   4

Love God with all your ___ ___ ___ ___ ___, ___ ___ ___ ___,
                       8   5   1   18 20   13 9   14 4

___ ___ ___ ___, and ___ ___ ___ ___ ___ ___ ___ ___
19 15 21 12   19 20 18 5   14 7   20 8

Love your ___ ___ ___ ___ ___ ___ ___ ___ as
          14 5   9   7   8   2   15 18

___ ___ ___ ___ ___ ___ ___ ___
25 15 21 18 19 5   12 6

Dear God,

Your Friend,

Week 4

God's Great Love

Leader/Parent Overview

Key Points:

- This week spend a lot of time talking about God's immense love for each person. If you can, tell each child individually that God loves him/her.

- In this chapter John speaks again on how a child of God doesn't sin. Remind the kids that we will sin but we don't do it on purpose or make a habit of it.

- Moreover, when we do sin God is ready and willing to forgive. A favorite example of mine is how we must clean our skin when it gets dirty. It is like that with sin. We get dirty on the inside from it and it needs to be cleaned. Tell God you are sorry and ask Him to help you work on not sinning. He is always ready to forgive!

Additional Questions:

- Why do you think John wants to remind us that God's kids don't make a habit of lying?

- How does knowing God loves you change the way you behave?

- Do you think that you should act differently being God's kid?

God's Great Love

Bible Reading

This week please read the following passage and write down three things you learn

1st John 3

1. _____
_____
_____
_____
_____

2. _____
_____
_____
_____
_____

3. _____
_____
_____
_____
_____

Taking a Deeper Look

This chapter has one of the greatest opening lines. It basically says "Look at how much God loves you by what He has given us, we can be God's kid!" The truth is Jesus died, was buried, and resurrected.[9] In this, He conquered sin and death.[10] In John 3:16 we are told that God so loved the whole world that He gave His son, so that those of us who will believe in Him will live with God forever. This offer is open to every person who has lived, is living, and will live. He extends the offer to all of us but it is our choice if we accept it.

1. Why do you think God wants each person to choose whether or not they accept His gift of salvation?

_____
_____
_____
_____
_____
_____

2. Have you accepted God's gift of salvation through Jesus? If so, when did you and what was it like? If not, do you have any questions you would like answered? Write them down.

_____
_____
_____
_____
_____
_____

You might be wondering what John means when he says that God's kids don't sin. He means that they do not continually choose to sin or participate in sinful behaviors. We will sin, and the Holy Spirit will convict us of our sin, and God will forgive us when we repent.

Jesus did more than conquer sin and death when He resurrected. Here in 1st John 3:8 we read how Jesus came to destroy the works of the Devil. The word Destroy means to render (to make) something inoperative.[11] This means when Satan tries to trick, tempt, or lie to you, you can just tell him to go away because you're covered in Jesus' blood and are on the winning side! You can overcome because of what Jesus has done for you.

3. What are some tricks, temptations, and lies that Satan has tried and said to you? How can you overcome them?

_____
_____
_____
_____
_____
_____

We will end this chapter with a lesson that we always need to be reminded of, no matter how old we get. We shouldn't love just through what we say but through our actions. Words only go so far. Many times a lot of people don't even mean what they say or keep their promises. God's children are held at a higher standard than those who aren't. We not only need to mean what we say, and keep our promises, we also need to live out what we say. In other words, we can say that we love others but our actions need to show it. Perhaps there is someone who is being bullied at your school and you can go to an adult and tell them about it so it can be brought to an end. Just saying you'll do it and not following through does nothing. However, if you do and tell an adult who can help take care of the situation, you're words and actions line up!

Seeing Z.O.E. Reflected in this Passage

Z - A part of being Zealous is making sure our talk and actions line up. What are some things you say you will do but haven't followed through with? What are some that you have followed through with?

_____
_____
_____
_____
_____

O - As God's kids we are to be Obedient and follow His commands. Read Exodus 20:1-17 and write down at least 3 of the 10 commandments. How can you be Obedient in following these?

_____
_____
_____
_____
_____

E - When we accept God's gift of salvation the Holy Spirit comes and lives inside of you. We can Expect that He will help us to live a godly life. How has the Holy Spirit helped you in your walk with God so far?

_____
_____
_____
_____
_____

Memory Verse

"So you also must consider yourselves dead to sin and alive to God in Christ Jesus. Let not sin therefore reign in your mortal body, to make you obey its passions."

Romans 6:11-12

We are dead to sin because Jesus came to render it inoperative in our lives. Although we still sin, how can you sin less often? When you sin, do you feel guilty? How do you feel when you ask for forgiveness?

_____
_____
_____

Being Z.O.E.

Our memory verse tells us to not allow sin to reign in our lives.

What do you think it means to allow sin to reign in your life?

_____
_____
_____

One thing it means is that we shouldn't let sin control us, or our behavior. Instead we should allow obedience to God and His commands to reign in our lives.

How can you let God and His commands reign in your life?

_____
_____
_____

God's Great Love

```
O M L S L W W Q J P K F B J O
C V B E N R R I X E W T J J B
C B E O Z X Y I N L E W Q U E
B R C R W F Q T K N Z Q P U D
G A W M C H K E F Q I J D S I
H N X O Z O K K V M D N B Q E
Q T E G R O M M V S T I G Y N
O D F B O D J E I A G S D S T
E X O D U S O R Q T Y B E H Y
N W N Q Q J V B Z A B H S G H
E W J J X T Z Y K N V U T N H
X L G X T L L G M E Q F R M D
F I N O P E R A T I V E O X R
P A C T I O N S G N N Z Y H P
M C P B N K Q B W L X R J C L
```

ACTIONS   DESTROY   EXODUS

INOPERATIVE   OBEDIENT   OVERCOME

SATAN   WINNING   WORD

God's Great Love

Across

1) Our words and _____ need to line up
3) Jesus came to _____ the works of Satan
5) People don't always keep their _____
7) God's Enemy
8) The word Destroy means to render _____

Down

2) God asks His kids to be _____ to His rules
4) Through Jesus' completed work we can _____
5) As God's kids, we are on the _____ side
6) What book are the 10 Commandments in?

God's Great Love

Directions: Match the numbers to the letters to reveal the answer

A	B	C	D	E	F	G	H	I	J	K	L	M
1	2	3	4	5	6	7	8	9	10	11	12	13

N	O	P	Q	R	S	T	U	V	W	X	Y	Z
14	15	16	17	18	19	20	21	22	23	24	25	26

___ ___ ___ ___ no other ___ ___ ___ ___ before ___ ___
 8   1   22   5   7   15   4   19   13   5

Do not ___ ___ ___ ___ ___ ___ ___ anyone/anything
        23   15   18   19   8   9   16

___ ___ ___ ___ ___ than ___ ___ ___
 15   20   8   5   18   7   15   4

Do not ___ ___ ___ ___ ___ ___ the ___ ___ ___ ___ of ___ ___ ___
        13   9   19   21   19   5   14   1   13   5   7   15   4

Remember the ___ ___ ___ ___ ___ ___ ___ day keep it ___ ___ ___ ___
              19   1   2   2   1   20   8   8   15   12   25

___ ___ ___ ___ ___ your ___ ___ ___ ___ ___ ___ ___
 8   15   14   15   18   16   1   18   5   14   20   19

Dear God,

Your Friend,

Week 5

A Time of Testing

Leader/Parent Overview

Key Points:

- I suggest that you read 2nd Peter 2 and Jude in preparation for this study. This week John tells us that every believer will have times of testing in their lives. Part of passing the test is knowing the Bible. In the above passages we are given several characteristics of false teachers. Perhaps you can write down a few that stand out to you and you can share and discuss them with the kids (i.e. they deny that Jesus is Lord).

- There are two main truths we need to continually reinforce: (1) The Gospel is that Jesus died, was buried, and rose again. (2) Jesus is the only way to Heaven.

- Express to them the importance of daily listening to or reading the Bible. Even if its only a couple minutes a day, the Word goes into the heart and stays. In times of difficulty and testing the Holy Spirit will bring Scripture back to our memory.

Additional Questions:

- What are some characteristics God's kids should have? Some examples would be love, joy, kindness, a servant's heart, etc.
- How much time do you spend reading or listening to the Bible?

A Time of Testing

Bible Reading

This week please read the following passage and write down three things you learn

1st John 4

1. _____
_____
_____
_____
_____

2. _____
_____
_____
_____
_____

3. _____
_____
_____
_____
_____

Taking A Deeper Look

When you are at school the teacher teaches you many things. Later on the teacher quizzes you on them and gives you tests. It is the same with the Bible!

God has given us the Bible and wants us to study it. There will be a day when we will be tested. The word test means to throughly examine.[12] These tests will come throughout your whole life, so never stop studying. Just as there are right and wrong answers on a test in school, there are also right and wrong answers for our test. The main one will be the Truth about Jesus. He died, was buried, and rose again.[13] Now Satan and his workers don't want people to know this Truth so he sends out his workers or spirits to cause confusion, deception, and division. For instance, there is a teaching that says Jesus was only a spirit and never actually took on human form. This is a false teaching because it goes against the truth of the Gospel. The Holy Spirit will help you when you are tested and will help you understand the Bible as you read it. Whenever you come across a teaching you are unsure of, ask an adult that is also one of God's kids and talk it out with them.

What do you know to be true about God? Where do you find these truths in the Bible?

_____
_____
_____
_____
_____

John encourages and reminds us that when we are tested we can win because of what Jesus has done for us. He says "greater is He that is in you than he that is in the world." The Holy Spirit is in all of God's kids and He is greater than any evil spirit that will come to test you. He will give you courage to face it, wisdom to understand the truth, and will show you where the testing spirit is in error. Just as the Holy Spirit uses us to spread the Gospel, Satan will use people who don't have the Holy Spirit to spread his lies.

Moving on, God is a great many things. One thing He is, is Love. It means that there is no hate in Him at all. God wants His kids to love one another. He doesn't want us to hate others or be jealous. We can love those we don't like by showing them kindness. It can be hard, but remember, God still loves those who don't like Him. God shows us His love in these ways: (A) Love is what He is, (B) Love is what He has done though Jesus' gift of salvation, and (C) Love is what He is doing through the Holy Spirit.

1. How can you show love to those you don't like or to those who don't like you?

_____
_____
_____
_____
_____

2. God shows His love toward us through the work of the Holy Spirit. How do you see Him working in your life today?

_____
_____
_____
_____
_____

Seeing Z.O.E. Reflected in this Passage

Z - God is love and He loves you. No matter what you do, He will always love you. He is Zealous to have a relationship with you because of His immense love for you. What does it mean to you to know that there is Someone who will always love you and want a relationship with you?

_____
_____
_____
_____
_____

O - We can be Obedient to study the Bible so we can be ready for the day we are being tested. Pick a book of the Bible and start reading every day. What book did you pick and why?

_____
_____
_____
_____
_____

E - Anytime we hear a false teaching or a lie about God we can Expect the Holy Spirit to alert us. Have you experienced this yet? What happened?

_____
_____
_____
_____
_____

Memory Verse

"For the word of God is living and active, sharper than any two-edged sword, piercing to the division of soul and of spirit, of joints and of marrow, and discerning the thoughts and intentions of the heart."

Hebrews 4:12

Even though the Bible was written over thousands of years, it is still applicable to us today. It is alive and active in that we can learn just as much through it today as Paul or John could have learned back then. How does the Bible still being relevant today prove that God is outside of time and that He is the only true God?

_____
_____
_____
_____
_____

Being Z.O.E.

This week as you read the Bible, write down three things that are true about God. Include the passage you found it in.

_____
_____
_____
_____
_____

A Time of Testing

```
I J O R B C O X I L O H E A C
E E M H W O A C T P T P Z O A
Y A Q S A M L O R E S L A I T
N L U B D T J N Z F S M W W J
Q O U R M P E F J G R T V L A
A U O O G N I U N I O B L K C
Y S X M V O S S W M Z N L V T
F E K Z D F U I H X M Q F X I
V V Q F U D X O R W D S I B V
B Q E W I C F N B N U R F H E
C U L Z W N I Q L M B R A J G
B I B L E O M Q O A U A C Q R
G L O V E Q O L Q N I X T V P
X E W G T C V S D E Z P G P H
G Q H X K O Q I G M Y O L I J
```

ACTIVE	BIBLE	CONFUSION
FACT	HATE	JEALOUS
LOVE	MAN	TEST

A Time of Testing

Across

3) There is none of this in God
5) Something that has been verified and confirmed
6) We must study this book to pass our test
8) Jesus was fully God and fully _____
9) This is something we are not to be

Down

1) This word means to thoroughly examine
2) This is something that false teaching will cause
4) The Bible is alive and _____
7) This is what God is

A Time Of Testing

Directions: Match the numbers to the letters to reveal the answer

A	B	C	D	E	F	G	H	I	J	K	L	M
1	2	3	4	5	6	7	8	9	10	11	12	13

N	O	P	Q	R	S	T	U	V	W	X	Y	Z
14	15	16	17	18	19	20	21	22	23	24	25	26

__ __ __ __ __ __ __ __ __. He has __ __
7 15 4   9 19   12 15 22 5   14 15

__ __ __ __ __ __ __ __ __
8 1 20 5   9 14 8 9 13

We can know __ __ __ __ __ when we __ __ __ __
              20 18 21 20 8   18 5 1 4

the __ __ __ __ __
    2 9 2 12 5

__ __ __ __ __ __ __ is He that __ __
7 18 5 1 20 5 18   9 19

__ __ __ __, than he that is in the __ __ __ __ __
9 14 13 5   23 15 18 12 4

Dear God,

Your Friend,

Week 6

Be Assured

Leader/Parent Overview

Key Points:

- We will be looking at eight assurances of our salvation. It would be good to go over the tenses of salvation with the kids.

- First we are justified, this happens right when we say yes to Jesus' free gift. We are then sealed with the Holy Spirit. This happens once.

- Secondly, we are sanctified. This is a life long process of being molded into the image of Jesus. As Christians we are to help each other along in our walks. Encourage the kids to help one another in their walks.

- Lastly, we are glorified. This will happen in our future. We no longer will have these human bodies but will have glorified ones.

Additional Questions:

- It would be fun to brainstorm with the kids on ways they could help each other in their walks. Maybe they could read the Bible together, help each other memorize Scripture, etc. If you have time, get a poster board and write all their ideas on it. This would be a very fun activity.

Be Assured

Bible Reading

This week please read the following passage and write down three things you learn

1st John 5

1. _____
_____
_____
_____
_____

2. _____
_____
_____
_____
_____

3. _____
_____
_____
_____
_____

Taking A Deeper Look

When I was your age I often wondered if I could be assured of my salvation. The simple answer is yes and here we find 8 assurances.

God is love. As His kid, His love is in you and works through you.

1. How do you see God's love in and through you?

_____

_____

_____

2. You're an overcomer. Jesus won the war between good and evil when He died and rose again. When you accepted His gift of salvation you went to the winning side.

_____

_____

_____

Jesus is God. We serve a Triune (3 in 1) God. God the Father, God the Son, whose name is Jesus, and God the Holy Spirit. There are witnesses here on Earth and in Heaven. Witnesses are important. It is Jewish custom that in order to have something confirmed there must be 3 or more witnesses.

3. Why is it important to believe that Jesus is God? What do you believe?

_____

_____

_____

You are promised everlasting life when you accept Jesus' gift of salvation. Remember when Jesus was crucified and the guilty man on one side believed in Jesus? Jesus told him "today you will be with me in paradise." The guilty man accepted the gift and one day in Heaven we will meet him. We are guilty of sin and when we accept Jesus' gift we can be assured we will one day be with Him in paradise.

God answers prayer! He gives us a variety of answers but he does answer His kid's prayers.

4. What are you praying about right now? Has God answered it?

_____
_____
_____

You live a life according to God's rules. When you sin, you come to Him and ask for forgiveness which He is ready and willing to give.

Sin and evil are things of this world that are contrary to how God wants us to live. These things should bother us and we need to avoid these things in our lives.

5. How do you avoid sin and evil when they come your way? Remember you're an overcomer so you can overcome these things!

_____
_____
_____

God is real and true. God is living. We should serve God and God alone. God should be number 1 in your life.

6. What does it mean to you to serve a living, true, and real God? How does this make Him more relational?

_____
_____
_____

Seeing Z.O.E. Reflected in this Passage

Z - One way we can show God how Zealous we are for Him is to not serve any idols. Idols can be anyone or anything who takes His place as number 1 in your life. Spend some time in prayer today and ask Him if there are any idols that need to be removed.

_____
_____
_____
_____
_____

O - As God's kids we represent Him wherever we go. How Obedient are you at showing others that you are His kid without having to use words. What kind of actions do you do that can express it?

_____
_____
_____
_____
_____

E - God answers prayers. We can Expect Him to answer! Sometimes He says yes, other times no, and many times just wait or maybe. Write about a time you prayed for something and God told you to wait. What did you learn during this waiting time?

_____
_____
_____
_____
_____

Memory Verse

"Let us hold fast the confession of our hope without wavering, for he who promised is faithful."

Hebrews 10:23

What does it mean to be faithful?

_____
_____
_____
_____

How has God proven faithful in your life?

_____
_____
_____
_____

Being Z.O.E.

This week your challenge is to have a purposeful prayer time for at least 20 minutes everyday. Mark if you prayed and write down what you prayed about.

Did God answer any of your prayers?

_____
_____
_____
_____
_____

Be Assured

```
R H O W B W Q J U O G D J N F
E R T E S L I V X Z X B E R P
P J S Q V H C Q I H P G S K R
E X G T X E Y K X N U B U P A
N F M G F R R D L W R A S Y Y
T B J Y G B Z Y A U P B T B E
I E B X P A H E O C O L T M R
N H P M A Y B E B N S B V T S
G Q M Q Q W H I K P E F L D Z
P D T H H X S L T D F H Q M P
X M V E E I I C K Q U W I O L
K M F B Y G K N L M L O D I A
G T Q N Y B D E B E L U O D T
N O V E R C O M E R Y N L F Y
H M S A L V A T I O N Z J F R
```

EVERYONE   JESUS   IDOL

MAYBE   OVERCOMER   PRAYERS

PURPOSEFULLY   REPENTING   SALVATION

Be Assured

Across

5) This is what you are because of what Jesus has done for you
7) God answers prayers with a yes, no , or _____
8) What is the name of God's Son?
9) Jesus' free gift is called _____

Down

1) Salvation is open to whom?
2) There is a difference between sinning accidentally and _____
3) Someone or something that takes God's number one place in your life
4) God answers all of these
6) When we tell God we are sorry for sinning we are _____

Be Assured

Directions: Match the numbers to the letters to reveal the answer

A	B	C	D	E	F	G	H	I	J	K	L	M
1	2	3	4	5	6	7	8	9	10	11	12	13

N	O	P	Q	R	S	T	U	V	W	X	Y	Z
14	15	16	17	18	19	20	21	22	23	24	25	26

__ __ __ __ __ __ __ through __ __
7 15 4 12 15 22 5 19   13 5

I'm an __ __ __ __ __ __ __ __ __ because of
      15 22 5 18 3 15 13 5 18

__ __ __ __ __
10 5 19 21 19

__ __ __ __ __ __ __ __ __ __
7 15 4 6 15 18 7 9 22 5 19

__ __ __ __ __ __ __ __ __ prayer
7 15 4 1 14 19 23 5 18 19

God is __ __ __ __, __ __ __ __, and
       18 5 1 12 20 18 21 5

__ __ __ __ __ __
12 9 22 9 14 7

Dear God,

Your Friend,

Week 7

Be Aware

Leader/Parent Overview

Key Points:

- This lesson falls in line with the one on 1st John 4. It would be good to review the lessons on being tested and characteristics of false teachers.

- Ask the kids who they think the most important woman in history is and why. You can give them these clues: She lived during Jesus' time, she has a sister, she had children, she is loved by all who believe in Jesus. The answer we're looking for is Mary, Jesus' mother.

- One point to emphasis is that John is reminding her of God's two greatest commandments. Even Jesus' mom needs reminding!

- Since we are partners with God we should tell others about God and encourage them to believe in Jesus. Work with the kids on how to share the Gospel: Jesus died, was buried, and lived again. Through this He conquered sin and death! When you accept His gift you too can be given everlasting life, be forgiven of sin, and live a life that makes God happy.

Additional Questions:

- In place of additional questions I highly encourage you to have the kids practice sharing the Gospel with each other. You're never too young to learn!

Be Aware

Bible Reading

This week please read the following passage and write down three things you learn

2nd John

1. _____
_____
_____
_____
_____

2. _____
_____
_____
_____
_____

3. _____
_____
_____
_____
_____

Taking A Deeper Look

This chapter has a bit of a mystery in it. It is our job to find the clues. It is written to the Lady Elect. The word elect means choice, select, successful, and excellent.[14] The clues throughout this letter tell us she has children, lives in Ephesus, and has a sister.

1. Starting with Eve up until until this letter was written, who do you think the most elect woman is?

_____

_____

_____

There are a lot of guesses out there. We are going on the thought that it is Mary, Jesus' mom. When Jesus died He asked John to take care of her.[15] There are several clues John gives us and she fits each one. Plus, she has been the most highly thought of woman in all of history. There are religions that only worship her, have shrines and buildings in honor of her, and so much more.

2. John opens by reminding the reader of the greatest commandments. Write down what those commandments are.

_____

_____

_____

The church in Ephesus was known for finding who the false teachers were and exposing their lies. They did a lot of great work. Their work is mentioned in Revelation 2:1-7.

Back then, there were no cars, planes, or trains. The mode of transportation was mainly walking or riding a donkey or horse. It could take days to get from place to place. By the time you arrived, you would be covered in dirt and sweat. Many times travelers asked to stay in people's houses in place of staying at an inn.

False teachers were known to the church in Ephesus because that church worked hard in exposing the lies these teachers taught. The false teachers often traveled. When they would come to Ephesus, they would ask to stay with one of the church members! Well, the members were watched by others in the community and they would think if they are taking in that teacher then maybe their teaching is ok. These false teachers were trying to create confusion and put the church members in a sticky situation.

3. Think about it - what would you have done? Keep in mind that we are supposed to be hospitable and love our neighbor as ourselves. Do you think it would be ok to take them in?

_____
_____
_____

Before we get into what John told them go, back to the first question. What are the two greatest commandments? Which one comes before loving our neighbor? That's right- Loving God with all of us! As God's kid you're His partner. You abide in Him, which means you continue to walk out His commands and you have a relationship with Him.[16] These false teachers are against God. They were abiding, or partnering with God's enemy and living a life that is far different from ours. Do you see the problem? They represent all that we stand against. The church in Ephesus would look like they were partnering with someone that is against what they believe.

4. Just as there were those in Ephesus who watched the church members to see what they would do, people watch us. They look to see if our walk and talk line up. How well do you represent Jesus in your daily living?

_____
_____
_____

5. John said it is important to not be friends with people of the world. This is because we live by God's rules and they don't. Be careful in choosing your friendships. Perhaps you can share the Gospel (Jesus died, was buried and resurrected[17]) with those who don't believe and you can lead them to the truth. It is important to be friends with some of God's others kids. We all can learn from one another, encourage each other in our faith, and so much more. Pray over your friendships and ask God if there is something He would have you change.

Seeing Z.O.E. Reflected in this Passage

Z - John was happy when he heard that there were those who were "walking in the truth". This is a way we can show God and others how Zealous we are for God. What are some examples of living out your faith?

_____
_____
_____
_____
_____

O - Jesus is our example of perfect Obedience. We will never be perfect like Him but the Holy Spirit will help us in living out an Obedient life. It doesn't matter how old we are or even who we are, we all need to be reminded to be Obedient in our daily living. How are you doing in this?

_____
_____
_____
_____
_____

E - God Expects and wants us to share the Good News of Jesus with others. In fact, Jesus commanded His disciples to go forth and share it![18] When was the last time you shared the Gospel with someone? What was the outcome?

_____
_____
_____
_____
_____

Memory Verse

"Walk in wisdom toward outsiders, making the best use of the time."
Colossians 4:5

As God's kids our behavior matters. How can you be wise in your behavior? When an opportunity arises for you to share about your faith, do you make the most of it or neglect it?

_____
_____
_____
_____
_____

Being Z.O.E.

This week read Second Peter 2 everyday. Each day write down one characteristic of a false teacher. This will help you when you are trying to discern the truth from the false.

Be Aware

```
L N C Z J W V V Z J X Q V H A
J V M O M M Y F W J P G E O U
E L R D N K A G T A D F H I F
S S E C E F F Z F E Z A U F A
U F V H K G U R A Y T U I A L
S H E G P Y O S A G M E Z I S
Q I L V O N O S I D L K M T E
O C A G S N Q M P O E B U H M
C T T F U F R A Q E N S W A A
H U I S M R K R F T L D N N M
E X O G K K E Y H E Z S K Y L
A O N P R V D W U B Q T E M T
Q Q V M E N Q U L T R U T H R
G Z R K J A O C U Y N K O Z J
E L E C T D Z J H C C U H M Z
```

CONFUSION	ELECT	FAITH
FALSE	GOSPEL	JESUS
MARY	REVELATION	TRUTH

Be Aware

Across

1) John took care of this woman after Jesus died
5) Many of this type of teacher traveled to Ephesus
7) Some of Jesus' half-siblings are walking in this
8) False teachers try to cause this
9) Means choice, select, successful, and excellent

Down

2) The church of Ephesus is also spoken of in this book of the Bible
3) We are to live this out daily
4) Who is the perfect example of obedience?
6) Another word for "Good News"

Be Aware

Directions: Match the numbers to the letters to reveal the answer

A	B	C	D	E	F	G	H	I	J	K	L	M
1	2	3	4	5	6	7	8	9	10	11	12	13

N	O	P	Q	R	S	T	U	V	W	X	Y	Z
14	15	16	17	18	19	20	21	22	23	24	25	26

__J__ __U__ __D__ __E__ gives us characteristics of __F__ __A__ __L__ __S__ __E__
10   21   4   5   6   1   12 19 5

__T__ __E__ __A__ __C__ __H__ __E__ __R__ __S__
20   5   1   3   8   5   18   19

They're __U__ __N__ __G__ __O__ __D__ __L__ __Y__   __M__ __E__ __N__   Verse 4
         21 14 7   15 4   12 25   13 5   14

They __D__ __E__ __N__ __Y__   __J__ __E__ __S__ __U__ __S__   Verse 4
      4   5   14 25   10 5   19 21 19

They __S__ __P__ __E__ __A__ __K__   __E__ __V__ __I__ __L__ of things they
      19 16 5   1   11   5   22 9   12

__D__ __O__ __N__ __T__ __K__ __N__ __O__ __W__   Verse 10
4   15 14 20 ' 11 14 15 23

They __B__ __O__ __A__ __S__ __T__ about themselves   Verse 16
      2   15 1   19 20

They __F__ __L__ __A__ __T__ __T__ __E__ __R__ others for their advantage   Verse 16
      6   12 1   20 20 5   18

Dear God,

Your Friend,

Week 8

Lessons from the Good and the Bad

Leader/Parent Overview

Key Points:

- Our behavior matters. We learn valuable lessons from three men.
- Gaius was a good guy. He is someone who encourages others.
- Diotrephes is a bad man. He is a bully and treats people with meanness. Talk about how this type of behavior isn't acceptable. When you see someone bullied you need to speak up.
- We don't know much about Demetrius. John felt the need to put him in the letter and say how he's been hearing great things about him. This tells us that others watch us and how we behave. Even when we think no one is watching, we had better be on good behavior.

Additional Questions:

- Do you watch how others behave? What have you learned from them?
- Why is it important to stand up for people who are bullied?
- Have you had any experiences with bullies?
- If someone were watching you, what do you think they would know about you through your behavior?

Lessons from the Good and the Bad

Bible Reading

This week please read the following passage and write down three things you learn

3rd John

1. _____
_____
_____
_____
_____

2. _____
_____
_____
_____
_____

3. _____
_____
_____
_____

Taking A Deeper Look

Our study is coming to an end as we go through John's last letter. Here we find three men. Two of them are good and one is bad. There are many lessons we can learn from all of them.

First, we have Gaius. He is someone who encourages others. He also loves to serve God through serving others. He lives out the commandments of God.

1. What does it mean to encourage someone? How can you encourage someone today?

___
___
___
___
___
___

2. In your life, who has encouraged you the most? Have you told them how thankful you are to them?

___
___
___
___
___
___

Next we have someone who is mean and a bully. Even though he behaves badly we can learn a lot from him about how not to live our lives. His name is Diotrephes. He has been known to gossip, not allow church members into the church, he is prideful, arrogant, and has even spoken poorly of John the Pastor. John tells us that when he gets back he is going to talk with him about his bad behavior.

3. What did you learn about the importance of our behavior?

_____
_____
_____
_____
_____

4. Why are gossip, pride, and arrogance bad?

_____
_____
_____
_____
_____

Last we have another good role model. We don't know much about him. However, John was hearing great things about Demetrius. So much so, that he felt the need to point out that he is doing good in his faith and walk with God.

5. Has anyone ever told you that your doing good in your walk with God? Has anyone encouraged you in your faith?

_____
_____
_____
_____
_____

Seeing Z.O.E. Reflected in this Passage

Z - Gauis proved how Zealous he was for the Lord through serving. Have you served in your church? If not, where do you think you would like to serve?

_____
_____
_____
_____
_____

O - We can learn a lot about disobedience through Diotrephes. How do his actions oppose how God wants us to live? How can you learn to be Obedient through his disobedience?

_____
_____
_____
_____
_____

E - God teaches us using many different ways. Just as our parents want us to learn, God does too. Since He is creative, we can Expect Him to use just about any experience to teach us something. What are some of the more creative ways God has taught you something?

_____
_____
_____
_____
_____

Memory Verse

"Teach me your way, O Lord, that I may walk in your truth; unite my heart to fear your name."

Psalm 86:11

This verse says "Teach me Your way, O Lord..." What are some ways of the Lord?

_____
_____
_____
_____

Have you ever questioned if something was from God? If and when you do, all you have to do is check it out in the Bible. He will never tell you to do anything that goes against His Word. Are you questioning anything now? Ask the Holy Spirit to help you find the answer in your Bible.

_____
_____
_____
_____

Being Z.O.E.

This week ask an adult you trust, and one of God's kids, for a report on how you're doing living out your faith. Write down some things they said.

_____
_____
_____
_____
_____

Lessons From the Good and the Bad

```
W G G D B D S Q W Y T K B D O
W F G A V C E F A D U K E I M
Q E Z O T W R B E B T Y H O V
X Q M E S M V X F Y P L A T T
H D Z X N S E V B N B P V R F
H L I A K C I R F D R M I E E
F L N M C Q O P C K R Y O P L
Z Q I L V U N U R K O K R H I
O T Y E G I E I R P Q L P E A
G T U W S S O F H A Q Z C S U
J A I M T K O L R A G T F R N
Y P I R B O Q J F R D E O V U
A G D U S R Y T H R E E Y M O
M T F L S J M T E O X I U E P
B D E M E T R I U S R Z S I W
```

BEHAVIOR   DEMETRIUS   DIOTREPHES

ENCOURAGE   GAIUS   GOSSIP

LIES   SERVE   THREE

Lessons From the Good and the Bad

Across

5) This matters!
6) How many letters did John write?
7) To help someone out
8) Diotrephes spread these about other people
9) Talking behind someone's back is

Down

1) To cheer up
2) Others spoke well of him
3) He served others
4) The troublemaker

Lessons from the Good and the Bad

Directions: Match the numbers to the letters to reveal the answer

A	B	C	D	E	F	G	H	I	J	K	L	M
1	2	3	4	5	6	7	8	9	10	11	12	13

N	O	P	Q	R	S	T	U	V	W	X	Y	Z
14	15	16	17	18	19	20	21	22	23	24	25	26

___ ___ ___ ___ ___ ___ ___ ___ ___ was given a
 4   5   13 5   20 18 9   21 19

___ ___ ___ ___ ___ ___ ___ ___ ___
 7   15 15 4   18 5   16 15 18 20

___ ___ ___ ___ ___ ___ ___ ___ ___ was a very
 4   9   15 20 18 5   16 8   5   19

___ ___ ___ person. His ___ ___ ___ ___ ___ got him into a lot
 2   1   4   1   14 7   5   18

of ___ ___ ___ ___ ___ ___ ___
    20 18 15 21 2   12 5

___ ___ ___ ___ ___ loved to ___ ___ ___ ___ ___, and
 7   1   9   21 19   19 5   18 22 5

he ___ ___ ___ ___ ___ ___ ___ ___ ___ many people
    5   14 3   15 21 18 1   7   5   4

Dear God,

Your Friend,

End Notes

1. Gen. 3:21.
2. 1 Peter 1:20.
3. 1 Cor. 15:3-4; Acts 1:9-11.
4. Word Study Again G509: From above. Being born again is being born from above.
5. Word Study Fellowship G2842: To partner with, partake of the spiritual blessings from God.
6. Word Study Advocate G3875: One who is called to one's aid.
7. Word Study Propitiation G2434: The act of appeasing wrath and conciliating the favor of an offended person.
8. Matthew 22:36-40.
9. 1 Cor. 15:3-4.
10. 1 Cor. 15: 54-57.
11. Word Study Destroy G3089: To render inoperative.
12. Word Study Test G1381: To scrutinize, to throughly examine.
13. 1 Cor. 15:3-4.
14. Word Study Elect G2959: Choice, select, successful, excellent.
15. John 19:26.
16. Word Study Abide G3306: To be continually operative in.
17. 1 Cor. 15:3-4.
18. Matt. 28:16-20.

Acknowledgements

Above all, I thank God, my Creator, the One who formed me for His purpose. Without Him, my life would be meaningless. I am ever so grateful for the gifts He has given me. To Him be all the glory, praise, and honor.

To my family: John and Fay, Jonathan and Shannon, Uncle Richard, Clayton, and Brickman. You are my rocks, my support, inspirations, the ones whom I can count on. I'm so blessed that God gave me you. Love you all.

To Darin and Debbie: Debbie, thank you for giving me the superhero name ZoeWoman so many years ago. Darin, thank you for designing the covers and the coloring pages. You made it all come to life with your artwork.

To Ruthie and Vi: Even though we are generations apart we are kindred spirits. I hope that in my senior years, I can be as wise as you are in the Bible. You reflect our Lord and Savior in every circumstance. You are amazing witnesses.

To Robert: Thank you for partnering with me in publishing. I thank you for your support, advice, and help throughout this process.

To Jan, Valerie, and Victoria: Thank you for being my eyes through the editing process. Ladies, you are a blessing in my life.

www.ingramcontent.com/pod-product-compliance
Lightning Source LLC
LaVergne TN
LVHW081355060426
835510LV00013B/1828